Palabras para adónde/ Where Words

Cerca y lejos

Near and Far

por/by Tami Johnson

Traducción/Translation:
Dr. Martín Luis Guzmán Ferrer

CAPSTONE PRESS
a capstone imprint

A+ Books are published by Capstone Press,
151 Good Counsel Drive, P.O. Box 669, Mankato, Minnesota 56002.
www.capstonepub.com

032010
005740CGF10

 All books published by Capstone Press are manufactured with
paper containing at least 10 percent post-consumer waste.

Library of Congress Cataloging-in-Publication Data
Johnson, Tami.
    [Near and far. Spanish & English]
    Cerca y lejos = Near and far / por Tami Johnson.
    p. cm.—(A+ bilingüe. Palabras para adónde = A+ Bilingual. Where words)
    Includes index.
    Summary: "Simple text and color photographs introduce basic concepts of near and far—in both English and
Spanish"—Provided by publisher.
    ISBN 978-1-4296-5337-4 (library binding)
    1. Orientation—Juvenile literature. 2. Space perception—Juvenile literature. I. Title. II. Title: Near and far.
III. Series.
BF299.O7J64318 2011
153.7'52—dc22   2010006593

Credits

Megan Schoeneberger, editor; Adalín Torres-Zayas, Spanish copy editor; Juliette Peters, set designer;
    Eric Manske, designer; Charlene Deyle, photo researcher; Laura Manthe, production specialist

Photo Credits

2004 George Hall/Check Six, 17; Capstone Press/Karon Dubke, 14, 15, 29 (bottom); Corbis/Bettmann, 6; Corbis/
Denis Scott, 26; Corbis/Frans Lanting, 8; Corbis/Jan Butchofsky-Houser, 13; Corbis/Joe McDonald, 20; Corbis/
NewSport/Andreas Neumeier, 7; Corbis/Owen Franken, 4–5; Corbis/Philip James Corwin, cover (bottom); Corbis/
Richard Hamilton Smith, 4 (foreground); Corbis/Roger Ressmeyer, 18–19; Corbis/Scott Stulberg, 12–13; Corbis/
zefa/Frank Krahmer, 28 (top); Corbis/zefa/Gary Salter, 16; Digital Stock, 10; Digital Vision, 9, 21; Getty Images
Inc./The Image Bank/Mike Brinson, 25; Getty Images Inc./The Image Bank/Steve Niedorf Photography, 24; James
P. Rowan, 28 (bottom); Minden Pictures/Pete Oxford, 22–23; Peter Arnold, Inc./Klein, 11; Shutterstock/Andy Lim,
29 (top); Shutterstock/David Woods, 29 (middle); Shutterstock/Johan Swanepoel, 27; Shutterstock/Mihhail Triboi,
cover (top)

Note to Parents, Teachers, and Librarians

Palabras para adónde/Where Words uses color photographs and a nonfiction format to introduce readers to
the vocabulary of space in both English and Spanish. *Cerca y legos/Near and Far* is designed to be read aloud
to a pre-reader, or to be read independently by an early reader. Images and activities encourage mathematical
thinking in early readers and listeners. The book encourages further learning by including the following sections:
Table of Contents, Fun Facts, Glossary, Internet Sites, and Index. Early readers may need assistance using
these features.

Table of Contents

Tabla de contenidos

People look bigger
when they are near.

Las personas se ven
más grandes cuando
están cerca.

People look like dots when they are far.

Las personas se ven como puntitos cuando están lejos.

When something is very
near to you, it's hard to
tell what it is.

Cuando una cosa está
muy cerca de ti, es
difícil saber qué es.

But when it is far enough away,
it's easy to see it's a frog.

Pero cuando está más lejos,
es fácil ver que es una rana.

When you are near an ostrich, you can see the fuzzy feathers on its head.

Cuando estás cerca de un avestruz, puedes verle las plumas peluditas de su cabeza.

When an ostrich is far from you, you can see its long neck and legs.

Cuando un avestruz está lejos de ti, puedes verle su largo cuello y sus patas.

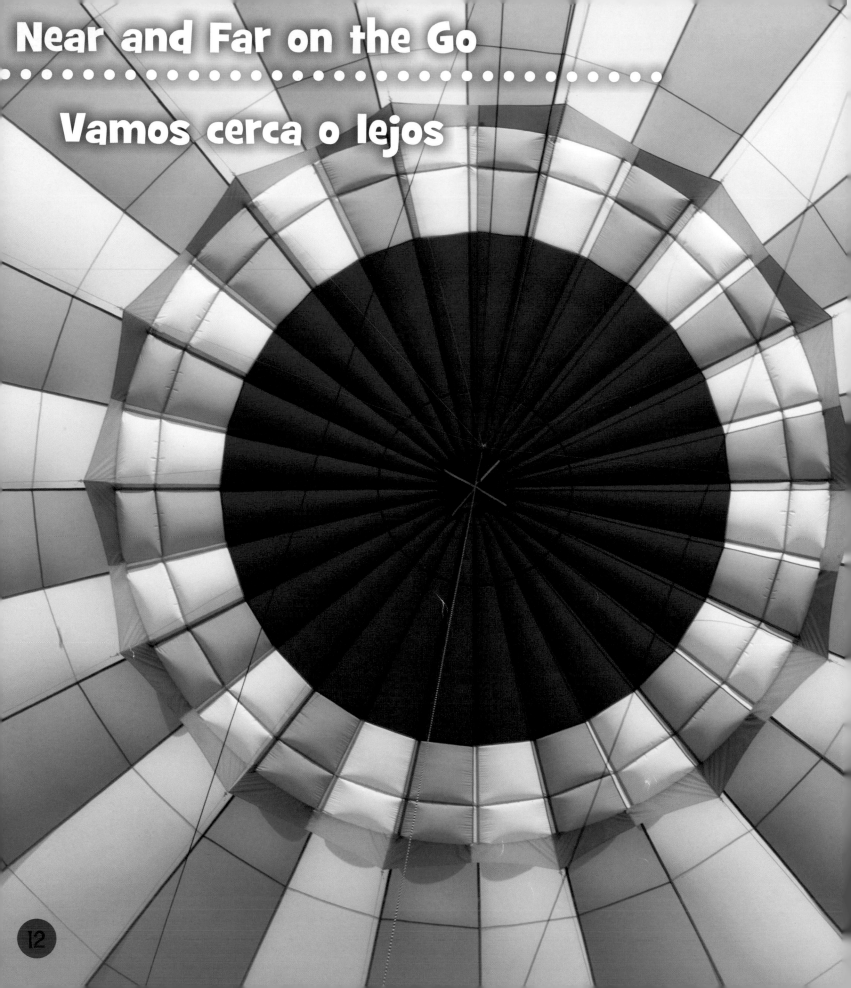

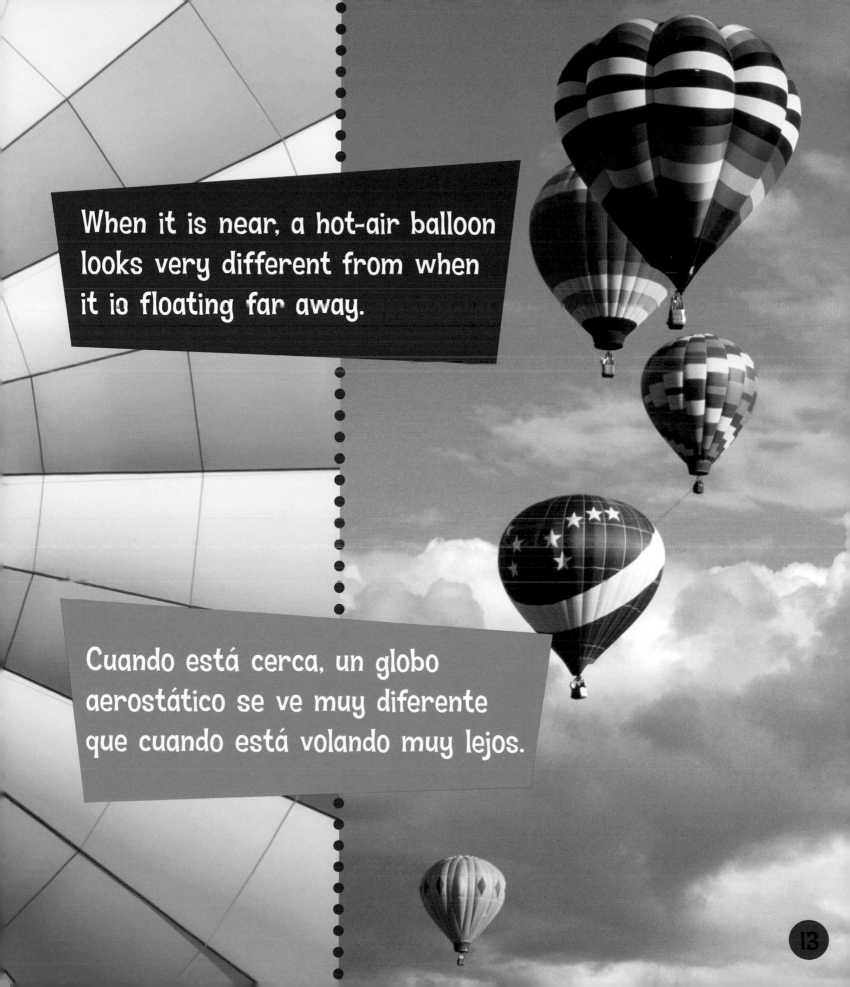

When it is near, a hot-air balloon looks very different from when it io floating far away.

Cuando está cerca, un globo aerostático se ve muy diferente que cuando está volando muy lejos.

Balloons stay near as long as you hold tightly to their strings.

Los globos se quedan cerca siempre que tengas el hilo bien detenido.

Let go of the balloons, and
they will float far away.

Suelta los globos,
y se irán muy lejos.

When you travel near your home, a bicycle is the way to ride.

Cuando paseas cerca de tu casa, la bicicleta es la forma de moverse.

For travel far away, an airplane is the way to go.

Cuando viajas lejos, el avión es la forma de moverse.

How far can something go?
Spaceships travel as far away as
anyone has ever been able to go.

¿Qué tan lejos puede ir una cosa?
Las naves espaciales viajan tan
lejos como alguien ha logrado ir.

What Is Better, Near or Far?
¿Qué es mejor, cerca o lejos?

Baby animals are safest
near their mothers.

Los animales bebés están
más seguros cerca de
sus madres.

Cape buffalo try to stay far away from hungry lions.

Los búfalos del Cabo tratan de mantenerse muy lejos de los leones hambrientos.

23

Some animals we like to have near us.

A algunos animales nos gusta tenerlos cerca.

Would you want to be near these animals? No, stay far away!

¿Te gustaría tener cerca a uno de estos animales? ¡No, que se queden muy lejos!

Near and Far Facts
Datos sobre cerca y lejos

Baby kangaroos, called joeys, stay very near their mothers. After birth, a joey crawls inside its mother's pouch. When the joey is about 8 to 10 months old, it is able to leave its mother's pouch and hop about.

_____

Los canguros bebés, conocidos como *joeys*, se quedan muy cerca de sus madres. Cuando nace el *joey* se mete a la bolsa de su madre. Cuando un *joey* cumple de 8 a 10 meses, ya puede salir de la bolsa de la madre y ponerse a saltar.

Baby sea turtles hatch on land and have to crawl far across the beach to reach their ocean home. Years later, many females return to the same beach to lay their own eggs.

_____

Las tortugas de mar bebés salen del cascarón en la tierra y tienen que arrastrarse por la playa para llegar a su hogar en el mar. Años después, muchas hembras regresan a la misma playa para poner sus huevos.

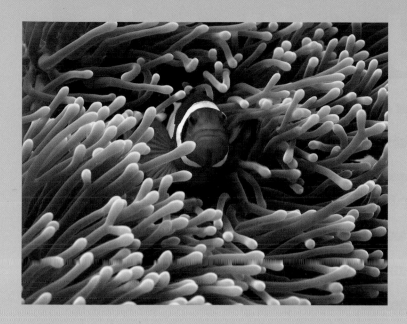

The clown fish stays near the sea anemone plant while other fish stay far away. The anemone's tentacles kill other fish that touch them. But the clown fish's body protects it from the anemone's deadly tentacles.

El pez payaso se queda cerca de las anémonas marinas, mientras que otros peces permanecen lejos. Los tentáculos de las anémonas matan a los otros peces cuando las tocan. El cuerpo del pez payaso lo protege de los tentáculos mortales de las anémonas.

The moon is nearer to Earth than anything in space. But it is so far away that you would have to travel all the way around the world more than 40 times to equal the distance from the moon to Earth. So, what do you think? Is the moon near or far?

La luna está más cerca de la Tierra que cualquier otra cosa en el espacio. Pero queda tan lejos que tendrías que viajar más de 40 veces alrededor de la Tierra para igualar la distancia entre la luna y la Tierra. ¿Así qué piensas? ¿Está la luna cerca o lejos?

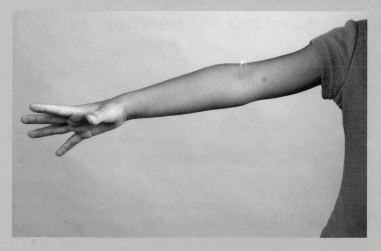

Something that is at arm's length is near. How many things can you reach out and touch right now? How many things are more than an arm's length away?

Algo que está a la distancia de un brazo está cerca. ¿Cuántas cosas puedes alcanzar y tocarlas en este momento? ¿Cuántas cosas están más lejos de tu brazo?

Index

Índice